Why Do Tectonic Plates Crash and Slip?

Geology Book for Kids

Children's Earth Sciences Books

BABY PROFESSOR

EDUCATION KIDS

Speedy Publishing LLC
40 E. Main St. #1156
Newark, DE 19711
www.speedypublishing.com

In this book, we're going to explain what tectonic plates are and why they crash and slip. So, let's get right to it!

WEGENER AND THE THEORY OF CONTINENTAL DRIFT

If you've ever looked closely at a globe, you might notice that if all the continents were pushed together they would fit like puzzle pieces with each other. If you look at a map of the underwater continental shelves, instead of the coastlines of the continents, it seems that the puzzle pieces fit even more closely.

Globe

Alfred Wegener

In 1912, an astronomer who was very interested in geophysics noticed the same thing. His name was Alfred Wegener. He proposed an amazing theory. He thought that at one time all the continents were one big landmass. He called this landmass "Pangaea," which meant "all lands."

He thought that this one big continent was all one piece until about 300 million years ago. During that time, which was called the Carboniferous period, the continents started to break apart and drift away from each other. This theory of how the continents moved was called "continental drift."

FOSSIL RESEARCH

Wegener began to do a lot of fossil research to determine if his theory could be correct. For example, if South America and Africa had been connected at one time, then animals and plants from that era should show up in the fossils of those continents. This proved to be true, but it wasn't enough scientific evidence to show that Wegener was right.

In his lifetime he proposed many ways that the continents could have moved. One of the ideas was that the Earth's mantle constantly undergoes so much heating and cooling at various times that it causes currents and pressure that could make the continents to drift apart.

In 1929, Arthur Holmes, a geologist in Britain, did more research on Wegener's heating and cooling theory. However, it wasn't until the 1960s that the idea of continental drift became more accepted. This acceptance came from many new discoveries, such as ridges and trenches in the ocean floor. Around 1962, two more scientists, Hess and Deitz, added their research to the theory of convection currents now known as "sea floor spreading."

Arthur Holmes

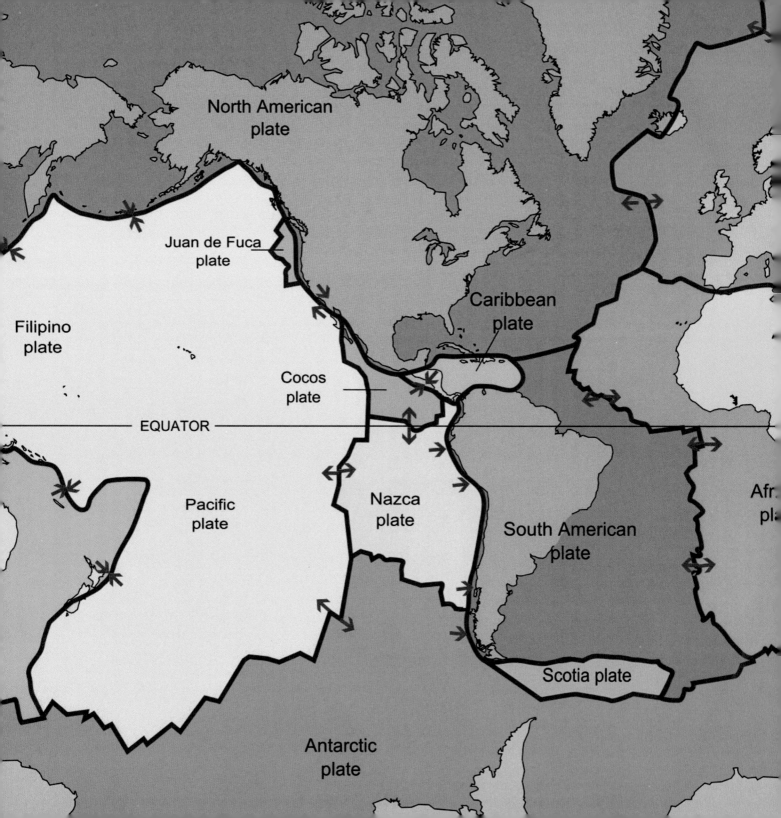

WHAT IS PLATE TECTONICS?

Plate tectonics is based on convection currents. You see a type of convection currents when you witness a pot of boiling water. When water is heated, it becomes less dense as its molecules spread apart, then it cools and its molecules come together making the water denser and it sinks again.

The process happens over and over again if water is heated on a stove. This convection is what causes the top of the water to erupt in violent bubbles when it boils. The same process is happening under the Earth's crust, only its liquid magma under there instead of water. Magma is hot, molten rock. When it bursts out of a volcano, it's called lava.

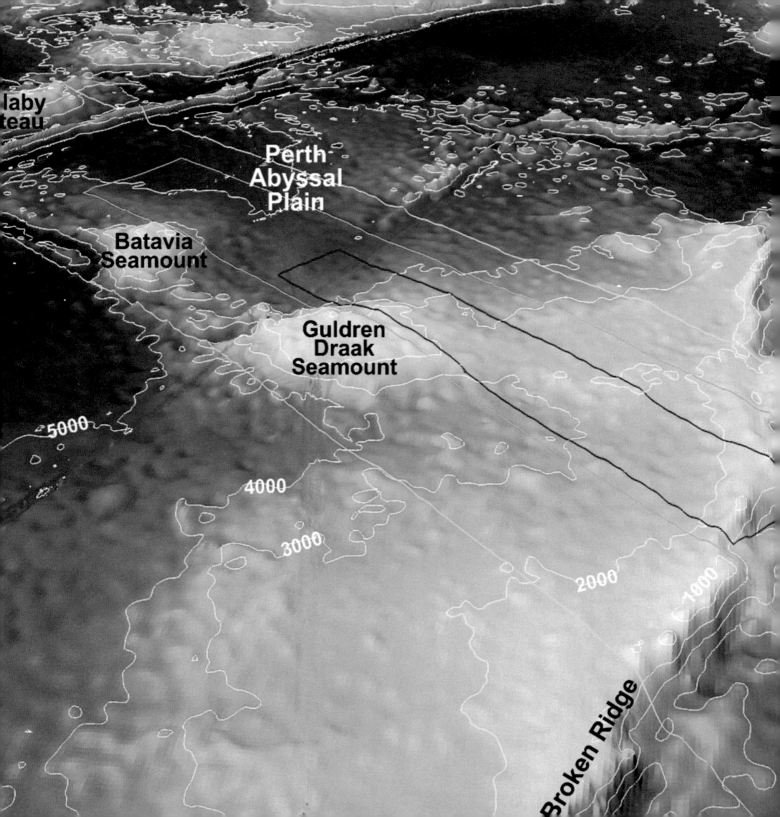

The Earth's surface is covered by a series of plates that form the Earth's crust. The ocean floors are constantly in motion. They spread, sink and regenerate. Convection currents from the magma under the Earth's crust create the heating and cooling cycle that pushes the massive plates in different directions. The source of heat that drives these currents is a radioactive process very deep inside the Earth's mantle.

LATES ARE MOVING UNDERNEATH YOU

If you traveled from the soil under your feet to deep inside the Earth you would go through many different layers. These many different layers fall into three categories. They are the crust, mantle and core. We live on the outermost layer, which is called the crust. Under the crust, there is hot magma and other rocks as well as minerals that are semi-solid. Eruptions of volcanoes and earthquakes are a result of convection currents from this intensely hot magma.

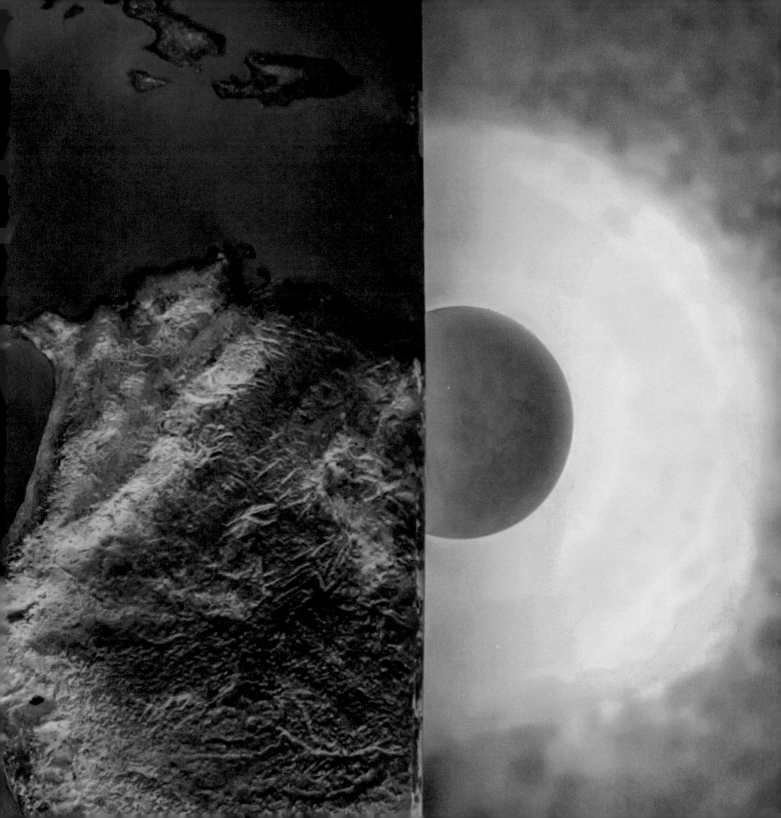

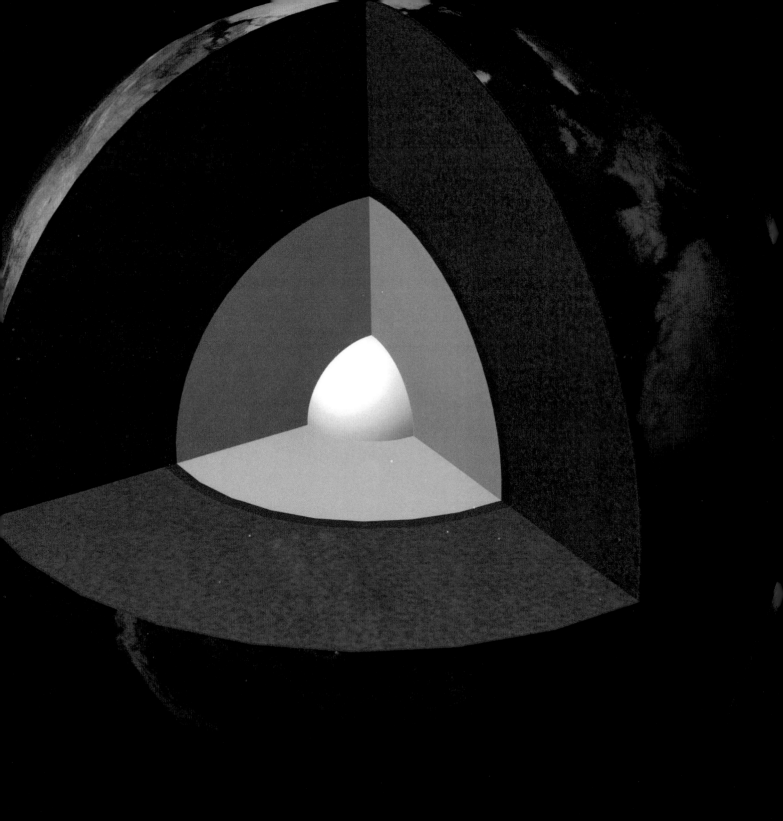

Under the mantle is the core of the Earth. It consists of minerals in an intensely hot liquid form. The temperature of this outer core is in the range of 7,000 to 9,000 degrees Fahrenheit. The part of the core that is deeper inside the Earth, its inner core, is mostly made of solid iron, but it's as hot as the Sun's surface which is about 10,000 degrees Fahrenheit. Even though it seems like the outer crust of the Earth is solid all the time, it's actually moving.

WHAT IS A TECTONIC PLATE?

A tectonic plate is a huge irregular piece of rock. The plate may be part of a continent or part of the ocean floor next to that continent. The size of a plate varies from thousands of kilometers to only a few hundred kilometers across.

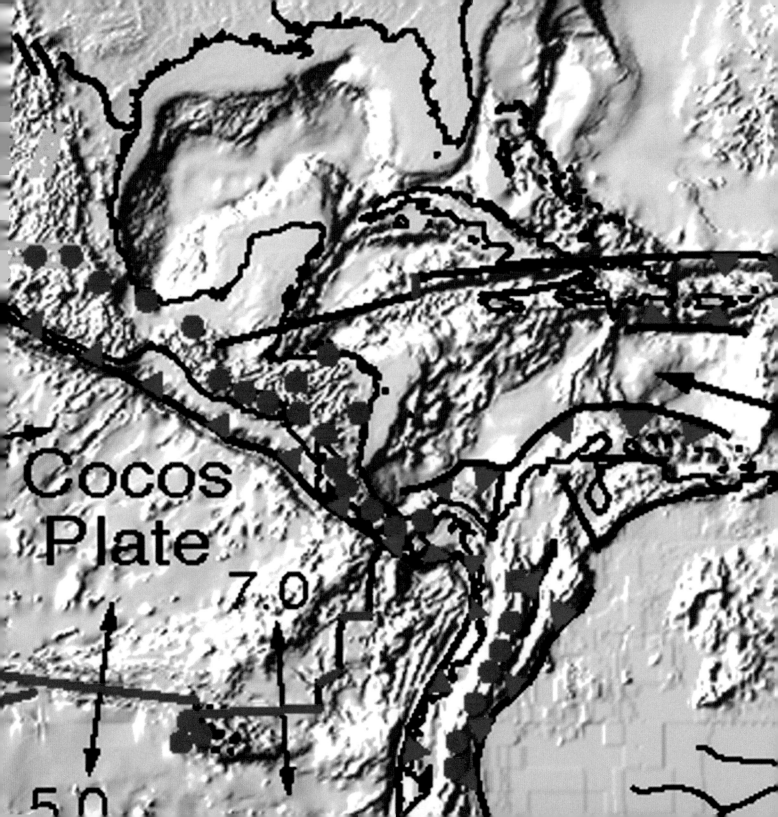

Cocos
Plate

7.0

50

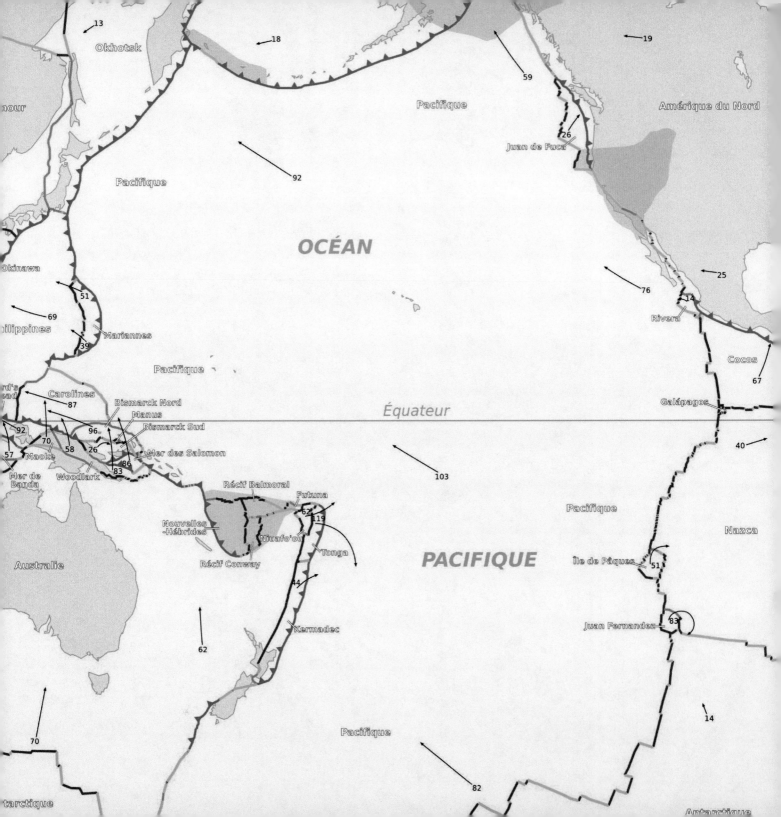

The Pacific plate and the Antarctic plate are some of the largest. The thickness of a plate also varies a lot. It ranges from about 15 kilometers thick to about 200 kilometers thick. For example, the middle of North America would be a thick plate.

HOW DO THESE MASSIVE ROCKS FLOAT?

So, how do these enormous plates of rock float since they have such huge weights? The reason has to do with what the rocks are made of. The crust of the continents is made of minerals that are mostly lightweight, like quartz and also feldspar.

Basaltic rock

The crust of the ocean is made up of basaltic rocks. These are much more dense and heavy than the rocks of the continental crust. Even though the continental crust is much lighter, it's usually much thicker, at least 100 kilometers thick. The oceanic crust is only about 5 kilometers thick. Continents are very deep in the Earth's crust to support the mountains that rise out of the Earth's surface. All the plates are riding on top of a hot, massive layer of magma.

We can't see most of the boundaries between the plates. Most of the boundaries are hidden underwater. However, with the help of GEOSAT satellites we can map them accurately from space. It's clear that most earthquakes and volcanoes are clustered near these boundaries.

GEOSAT Satellite

Scientists believe that tectonic plates formed very early in Earth's history and have been drifting around on the surface like bumper cars that bump, cluster and separate again.

Plates alter over long periods of time. This is happening right now off the coast of the states of Washington and Oregon. A small oceanic plate called the Juan de Fuca is sinking under the continental North American Plate.

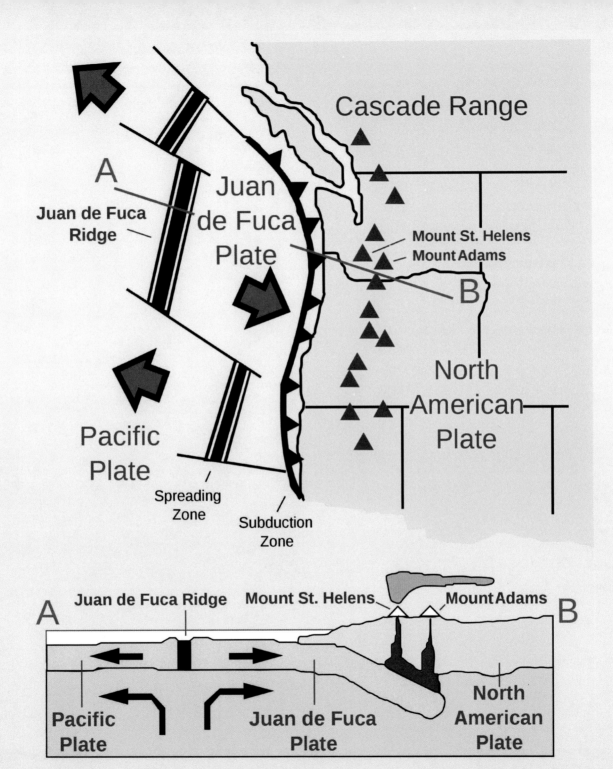

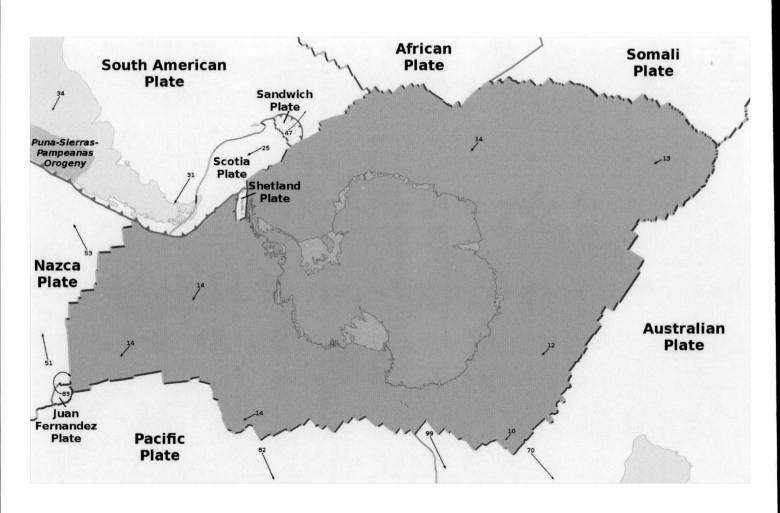

HOW MANY PLATES ARE THERE ON THE EARTH?

There are eight major plates on the Earth's surface. There are also lots of minor plates. We don't see this movement taking place because these massive pieces of rock are only moving a few centimeters every year.

It takes millions upon millions of years for the landmasses to move apart a significant distance. However, if you were ever in a very severe earthquake, you might feel the earth rolling under your feet, so you would know that the earth's plates do move!

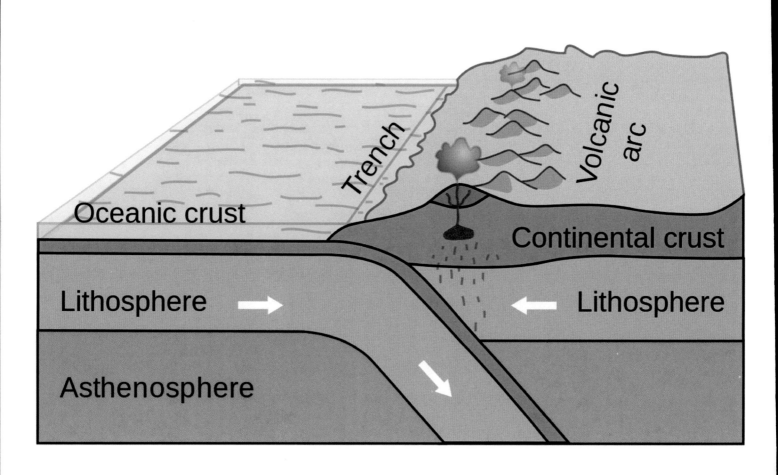

THE LITHOSPHERE AND THE ASTHENOSPHERE

The tectonic plates are on the first layer of the Earth called the lithosphere. This is the crust and part of the mantle. Directly under the lithosphere is the layer where the convection currents are created. It's called the asthenosphere and it is a hot flowing part of the Earth's mantle made of molten rock called magma.

All the rock, both solid and liquid, inside the Earth is constantly giving off both heat and radiation. This is what heats rocks, melts them and solidifies them again. The plates are floating on top of these convection currents.

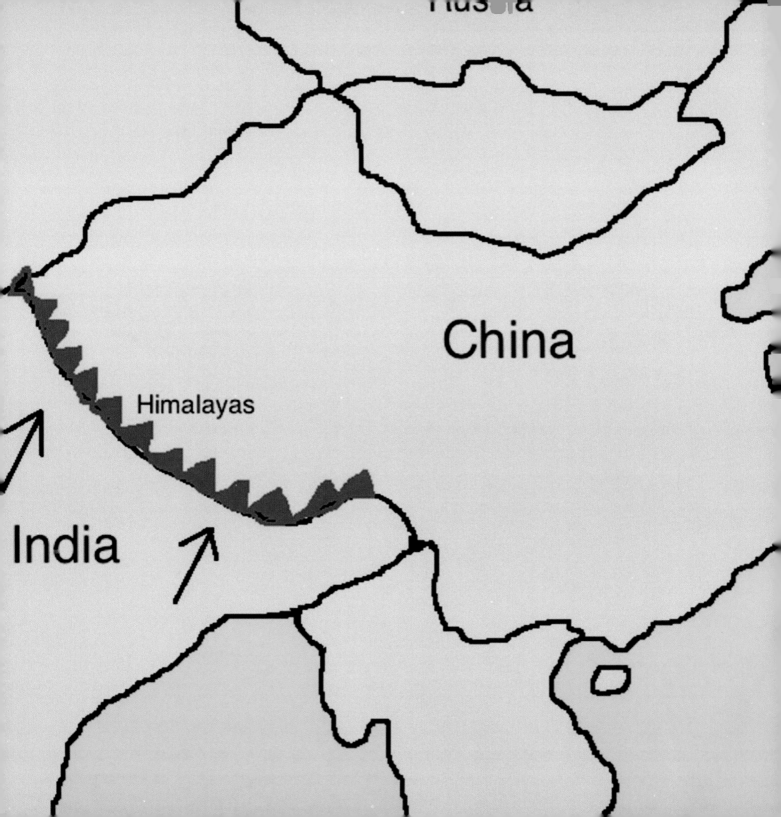

When the tectonic plates float apart it's called a spreading center. When the plates are moving together with each other it's a subduction zone. Sometimes the force is so powerful that two plates are forced into each other in what's called a zone of convergence. They can't occupy the same space at the same time so one moves under the other.

When one plate moves down into the asthenosphere, the heat from the molten magma causes it to begin to melt. The place where the plates meet forms a huge crack or trench in the Earth. Some of the deepest regions of the oceans are made up of these trenches.

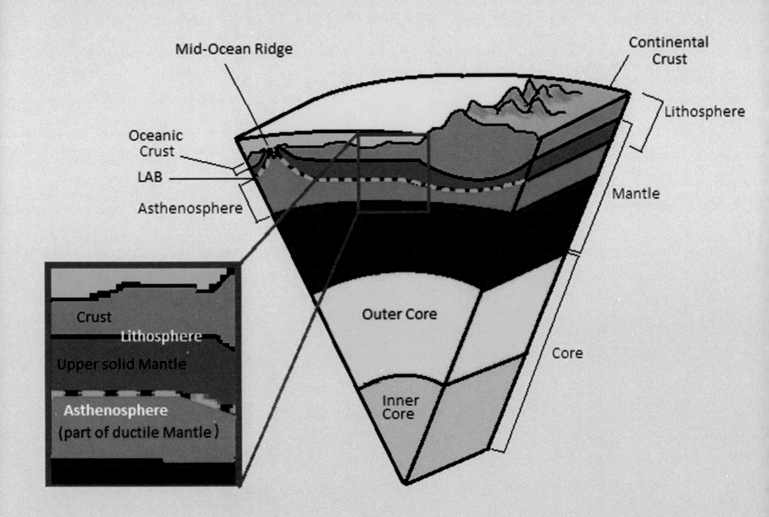

PLATE BOUNDARIES

The movement of the plates can be researched best at the boundaries between the plates. There are three major types of plate boundaries.

- Convergent Boundaries are where two plates are pushing together.

- Divergent Boundaries are where two plates are pushing apart.

- Transform Boundaries are where two plates are sliding past each other. These locations are called "faults" and earthquakes occur at these faults frequently.

One well-known Transform Boundary is the San Andreas Fault located in Northern California. It is the boundary between the Pacific Plate and the North American Plate. This fault is responsible for many of the earthquakes that take place in the region.

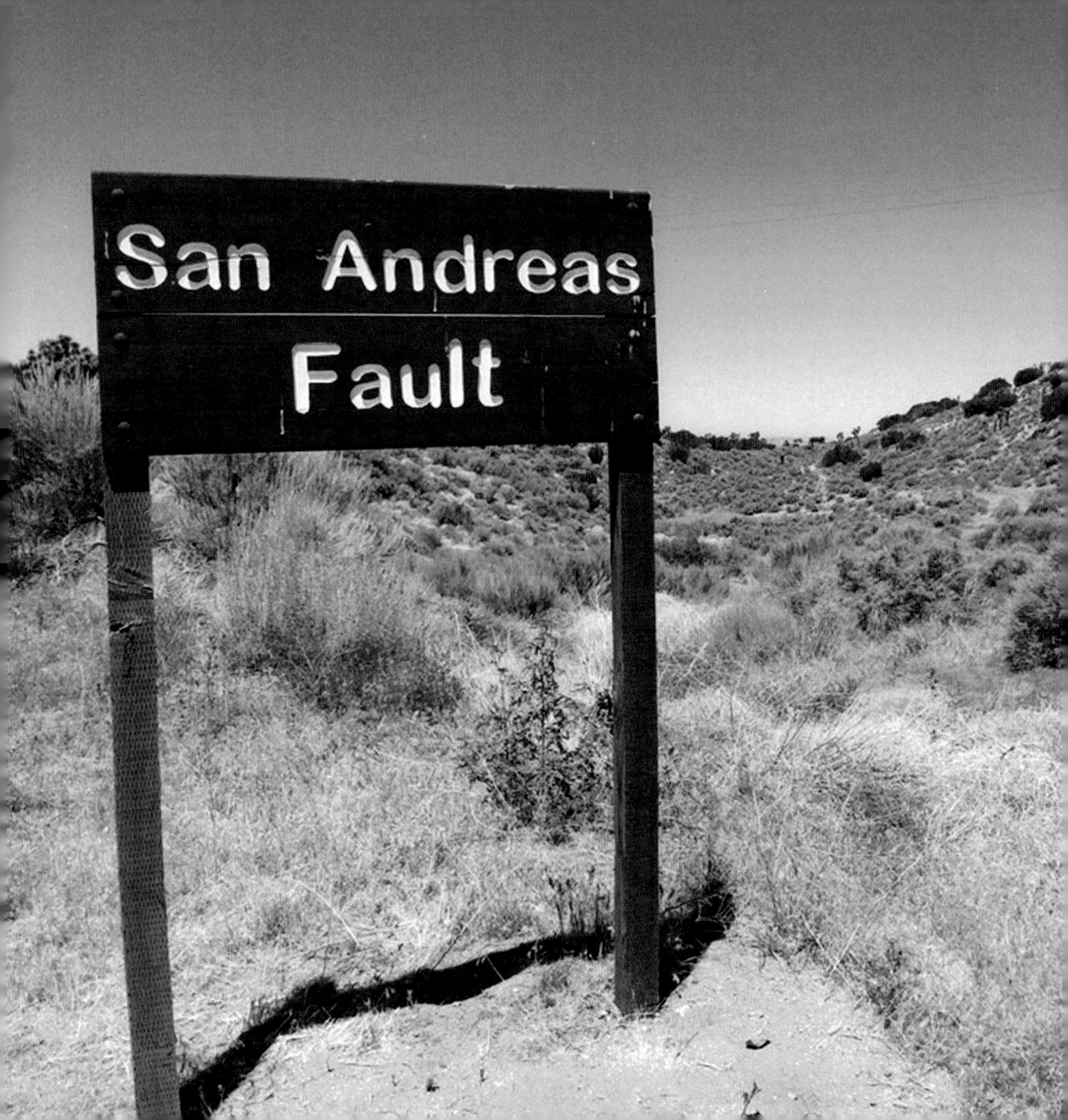
San Andreas
Fault

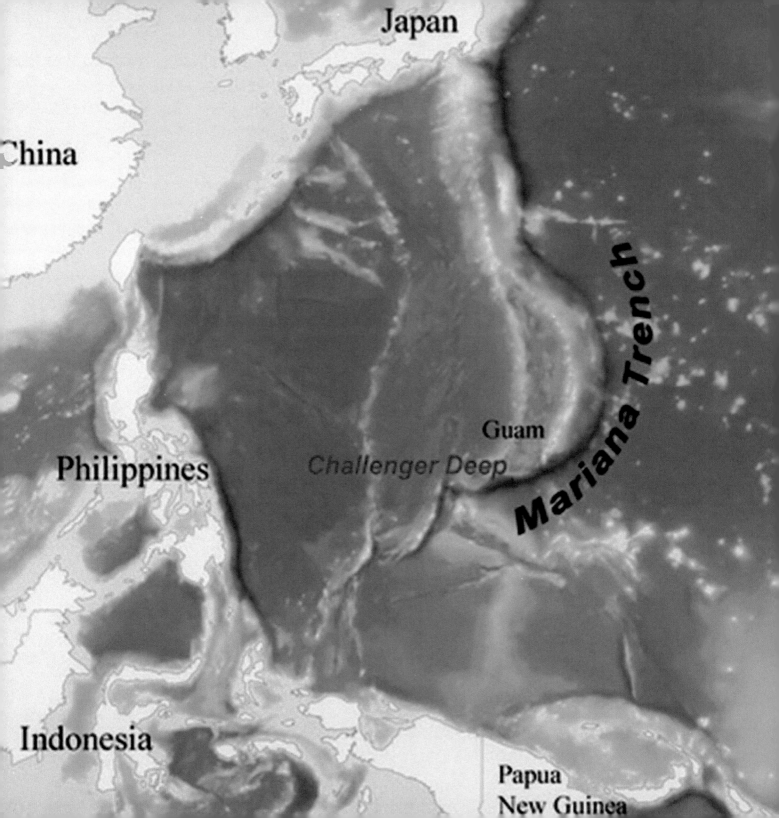

China

Japan

Philippines

Guam

Challenger Deep

Mariana Trench

Indonesia

Papua
New Guinea

Formed by the Convergent Boundary between the Pacific and Mariana Plates, the Mariana Trench is the deepest part of the ocean.

Thanks to GPS, scientists can now track the movement of all the tectonic plates on Earth.

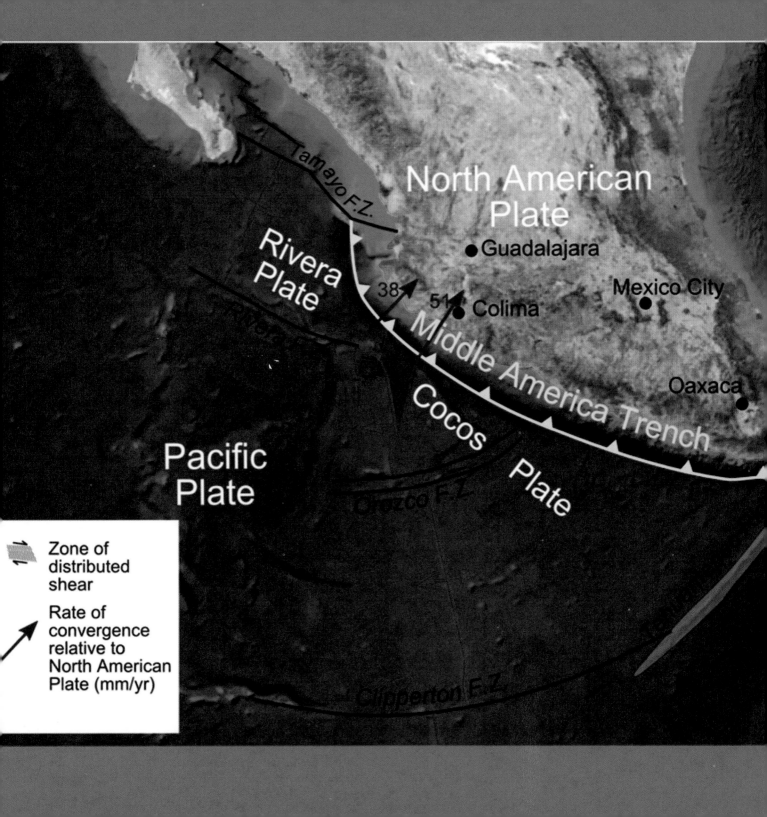

Awesome! Now you know more about the process of how and why tectonic plates crash and slip. You can find more Geology Books from Baby Professor by searching the website of your favorite book retailer.

Visit

BABY PROFESSOR
EDUCATION KIDS

www.BabyProfessorBooks.com

to download Free Baby Professor eBooks
and view our catalog of new and exciting
Children's Books